This library edition published in 2013 by Walter Foster Publishing, Inc.
Walter Foster Library
3 Wrigley, Suite A
Irvine, CA 92618

Printed in Mankato, Minnesota, USA by CG Book Printers, a division of Corporate Graphics.

First Library Edition

Library of Congress Cataloging-in-Publication Data

Lee, Jeannie, 1983-
    Manga / by Jeannie Lee.
        pages cm. -- (How to draw & paint)
    Includes bibliographical references and index.
    1. Comic books, strips, etc.--Japan--Technique. 2. Cartooning--Technique. 3. Comic strip characters--Japan. I. Title.
    NC1764.5.J3L44 2013
    741.5'1--dc23
                                                                            2013012505

052013
18134

9 8 7 6 5 4 3 2 1

My Manga World

Author Jeannie Lee always had an affinity for comics and cartoons—she grew up with Korean comics (man-hwa) as a child and was a devoted Disney fan. When she first discovered Japanese manga and anime, however, she knew she was hooked for life. Jeannie started drawing at a very young age, and her supportive parents found a talented local contemporary Western artist by the name of Ji Young Oh, who took Jeannie under her wing for over seven years. Jeannie considers Ms. Oh to be the most important artistic influence in her life. Her education also included two years of studying traditional character animation at California Institute of the Arts; from this education spawned interests in Flash animation and working with vectors. Jeannie considers herself very fortunate to be able to indulge in many types of artistic expression and plans to continuously increase her skill set in the years to come. Currently, Jeannie is a digital artist at Gaia Interactive, and she has worked for Marvel Entertainment, Inc., TOKYOPOP, and UDON Entertainment. When she isn't working, she indulges in various crafts and hobbies, such as knitting.

CONTENTS

The Art of Manga 2
Materials 3
Basic Shapes 4
Shading 5
Composition 6
Drawing Heads 8
Drawing Hair 9
Drawing Facial Features 10
Full Figure Male 12
Full Figure Female 13

Different Body Types 14
Male Hero 16
School Girl 18
Ninja 20
Basic Manga Principles 22
Choose Your Own Adventure 24
Manga Meet & Greet 26
Finding Inspiration from Real Life 28
Manga-fy This! 30
Conquer the Manga-Verse 32

The Art of Manga

Manga is the Japanese word for "comics," which literally translates to "whimsical pictures." It is generally used to describe comics that are made in Japan, but it is also loosely used to describe comics that resemble Japanese comics, even though they are not created in Japan. The four major types of manga are *shônen*, *shôjo*, *seinen*, and *jôsei*. *Shônen*, or boys' manga, is action-packed and usually includes sports, science fiction, or fantasy elements. Dealing with romance, comedy, and coming-of-age drama, *shôjo* manga is aimed at junior high school and high school-aged girls. Adult male audiences read *seinen* manga, which offers business and crime stories, as well as historical and military dramas. And for young and middle-aged women, *jôsei* manga focuses on career, family, and romantic dramas. There are also manga for food enthusiasts, gamers, and other hobbyists.

Most manga is produced in Japan and translated for overseas audiences, but original manga and manga-influenced works can increasingly be found in Korea, China, France, and America as well. Discover the art of manga with the instruction in this book, produce your own manga, and become a part of the growing global manga community!

Tip

In Japan, a *mangaka,* or manga author, has assistants who help with details, backgrounds, and screentone. Most manga artists start off as assistants before attaining full *mangaka* status, but it is possible to gain recognition through contests and skip the apprenticeship stage. You too can become a *mangaka!*

Materials

...re are the basic materials you'll need to begin creating your own manga.

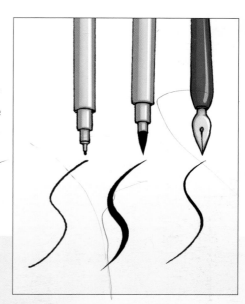

...ncils

...HB pencil is great for beginners, but you may ...o want to try out the other lead types, which ...y in hardness and value. Try a non-photo blue ...ored pencil for initial sketches and be sure to ...ep your pencils sharp. Use a rubber eraser to ...an up mistakes and unneeded pencil lines.

...ns

...e an ink pen if you want to ink your drawings. ...can also experiment with different types of ...s, such as dip, brush, and ballpoint pens for ...erent effects. It is recommended to use ...terproof ink for more permanent results.

...lers

...draw borders and straight lines, use a ...ndard 12" ruler. Consider purchasing a ...ngle ruler, protractor, or stencils for various ...es of lines and curves. When inking, use a ...er with an inking edge for cleaner drawings.

Coloring Tools

Color your drawings with markers, colored pencils, or digital coloring.

Paper

Use a sketchbook to thumbnail your ideas and start recording your own manga chronicles. It may also help to use comic layout paper with pre-printed borders. For more finished drawings, use a heavier white paper with a smooth finish, such as Bristol board.

Screentone

You may want to purchase pre-printed screentone patterns to add texture and shading to your artwork. Cut out the screentone, peel off the protective backing, and place the screentone on your drawing. Next, adhere it to the paper by firmly rubbing with a burnisher. Remove excess screentone with a screentone eraser.

Using Different Pens Use a fine-tipped pen for smooth, consistent lines. To emphasize elements in an image, go over them with a bold brush pen. Dip pens are fun because you can create a wide variety of line widths with just one tip, depending on pressure, or how hard you push down as you draw.

Inking Edges

An inking edge provides a gap between the ruler and paper, preventing ink from bleeding into the paper. If you can't find beveled rulers with inking edges, make your own by taping pennies to the bottom of your ruler.

Raised beveled ruler

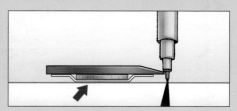

Creating your own beveled ruler

Basic Shapes

Before drawing anything, an artist must first understand the basics. Any image—from a photograph of a live model to a character out of your favorite manga—can be deconstructed, or broken down into a series of basic shapes and lines that make up the overall form. Use basic shapes, like circles, squares, and cylinders, to create your character's form. Breaking down complex drawings to basic shapes helps artists understand why certa[in] shapes and forms move the way they do. It also helps to easily identify areas that need correction when it comes to proportion, or foreshortening, which can be complex. However, don't get caught up in the details; the idea is to learn how to build a figure from the bottom up, one step at a time.

Step 1
Start with a basic skeletal structure. Identify the head and joints with circles, and major body parts with lines that establish the pose. Height and proportion should be established at this point.

Step 2
Lay down the basic shapes by using your first line structure as a guide. Use simple shapes like circles and cylinders to flesh out your figure.

Step 3
Continue defining the details of your figure, including the clothing. Having a rough sketch of the body on which to draw the clothing should make it easier.

Step 4
Add your character's facial features, hair, and clothing details. After finalizing the details, ink the outline of your drawing.

Step 5
Now color your drawing.

Tip
A good exercise is to study a few pages in your favorite manga and try deconstructing each character into basic shapes. Eventually, you will be able to deconstruct just by looking, without having to actually sketch it out!

Shading

Once you have established the basic shapes and details of a drawing, you can add depth to the forms with shading. Create the illusion of three-dimensionality in a two-dimensional object with clear contrasts in *value*, or the relative lightness or darkness of a color or black. Pay attention to the value gradations in the lights and shadows of the egg at right and the final, colored image below. You can shade a drawing with pencil, ink, screentones, or any medium used to color.

Hatching The most basic method of shading is to fill an area with hatching, which is a series of parallel strokes.

Light and Shadow

The *highlight* is the lightest value, where the light source (see page 6) directly strikes the object. The *light gray* area surrounds the highlight, and the *middle gray* is the actual color of the egg, without any highlights or shadows. The *cast shadow* is the shadow that the egg casts onto the ground. The *form shadow* is the shadow that is on the object itself. *Reflected light* bounces up onto the object from the ground surface.

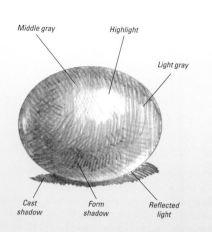

Middle gray   Highlight   Light gray   Cast shadow   Form shadow   Reflected light

Coloring

When coloring, work in layers—from the lightest colors to the darkest shadows. Be sure to make all your strokes in the same direction and leave the brightest highlights white. Use markers to achieve a blocky coloring style common in *anime*, or Japanese animation. You may also try colored pencils, which work similarly to regular pencils, or digital coloring techniques for blending and various lighting effects.

Inking

Inking is the term used for creating line art, or using a pen or other ink material to finalize a drawing. Inking will preserve your drawings. When inking, varying the line widths creates the illusion of texture, and can help give depth to your drawing. You can start with a black marker, but you'll also want to experiment with different pens. Dip pens have interchangeable tips and brush pens produce bold lines. Try ink pens for more consistent ink flow or ballpoint pens for softer, subtle line art.

Dip Pen

Brush Pen

Ink Pen

Ballpoint Pen

Composition

Before beginning a drawing, think about the image as a whole—the format, perspective, focal points, and lines. As every panel in manga tells a part of a story, it's helpful for you to think about the flow and theme of your drawing and what you want to accomplish as a whole. Consider portrait, landscape, and other format shapes as well as different perspectives for a range of visual effects. To direct the viewer's eye through a drawing, include focal points, or areas of interest, and use a variety of lines to capture mood and action. Planning out these elements early on will prevent major revisions later in the drawing process.

Compelling Compositions **In both drawings, the characters' eyes and weapons are powerful focal points. The folds in the assassin's robe lead the viewer's eye through the first picture, with radiating diagonals suggesting action. The second image uses sweeping hair curves and sketchy lines in the foreground arm to imply movement and highlight the poised ninja star.**

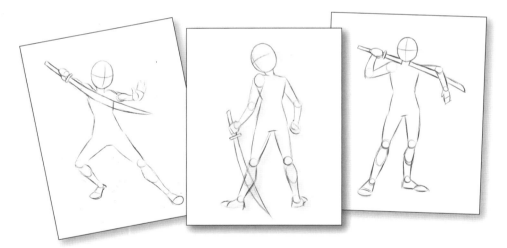

Creating Thumbnails As you brainstorm potential formats, perspectives, focal points, and lines for your drawing, create thumbnail sketches to help you visualize everything as a whole. Decide whether to zoom in on an area of the character with a cropped close-up or to include the full figure. Think about the position of the figure on the page and experiment with different poses. The purpose of drawing thumbnails is to give yourself a snapshot of your final drawing—a visual map that you can follow and use to work out various complexities, such as composition and poses. They should be quick and loose so that ideas can flow freely.

Light Sources

As you work out your composition, decide where the light source will be placed in your drawing. The direction and intensity of light affects how your subject's form appears and influences the mood of a scene. As the light source moves, so do the highlights and shadows. Pay special attention to the light source when shading your drawings (see page 5 for more information on shading). Notice the areas of reflected light in the three-quarter lit and backlit diagrams. Reflected light separates large areas in shadow and adds depth to an image.

Three-Quarter Lighting This light source creates bright highlights and dramatic shadows for greater depth.

Top Lighting This figure is lit from directly above. Top lighting is perfect for scenes set at high noon.

Back Lighting Backlit subjects often have a halo effect with illuminated edges and silhouetted forms.

Lines of Action

Different types of lines in a composition, such as curves or diagonals, can convey action and movement. However, the line of action is a specific, imaginary line that extends through the main portion of the figure you are drawing, usually following the direction of the figure's spine. The line of action, along with two smaller lines—the shoulder line and the hip line—define a figure's pose. It is also helpful to plan out the facial feature guidelines on the head and the four major joints in your initial sketch. These structures will allow you to quickly and efficiently establish a character's pose. A good exercise for understanding how these interrelated lines and joints make up a pose is to observe a live, human figure—your own body! Take several different poses in front of a large mirror and sketch out the line of action, shoulder line, hip line, major joints, and facial guidelines.

Line of Action The blue line of action above mimics the spine and the tilt of the neck and head. Defining the line of action first will help you figure out the rest of the pose, since all body parts follow the orientation of the trunk and spine.

Shoulder and Hip Lines The shoulder and hip lines intersect the line of action and define the position and origin of movement for the limbs. Establishing these lines with the line of action offers base for how far the limbs can move in any direction.

Tilting Lines Tilt the shoulder and hip lines in opposite directions to achieve more interesting and natural-looking poses. Doing so adds a subtle dynamic to the pose, when compared to a character whose shoulders and hips are parallel to the ground.

Perspective

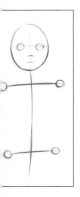

Front View
From the front view, with a subject simply standing facing forward, the hip and shoulder lines are parallel and the four major joints are equal in size. In males, the shoulder line is generally longer than the hip line, since males tend to have broader shoulders than females.

Three-Quarter View In this diagram, the figure is at a three-quarter angle, which is the most commonly drawn perspective. Notice that the shoulder and hip joints (red circles) closest to the viewer are larger than the joints on the farther side. (See page 12 for more on this effect.)

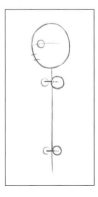

Side View
The side view is often difficult to draw, because only the line of action and joints closest to the viewer are visible. I suggest drawing through the image and placing all lines and joints. Your final drawing will appear more three-dimensional if you can visualize the entire structure.

Drawing Heads

The head is probably the most important body part to draw, as it is the source of a character's emotion and personality. Study the diagrams of the male and female heads at right for average ratios and proportions between facial features. Some artists draw in a more realistic style with facial proportions that are closer to the real human form; other artists choose to draw in a more stylized way with bigger eyes or longer foreheads. Once you understand the fundamental shapes and proportions of a typical realistic face and its features, you can bend the rules to create more extreme or unique styles.

Naturalistic

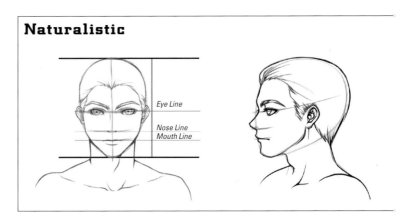

Eye Line
Nose Line
Mouth Line

Stylized

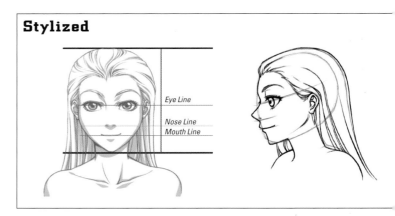

Eye Line
Nose Line
Mouth Line

T-Zone A simple yet efficient way of measuring eye distance is to use the eye itself. Generally, the space between the eyes is about the length of one eye. There is a similar amount of space between the bridge and tip of the nose. However, these are only average measurements—your style may dictate otherwise!

Step 1
To draw a head, begin with the head shape, which is usually an oval. See "Head Shapes" on page 11 for examples of different head shapes.

Step 2
Once you have established the face shape, sketch in the guidelines for the facial features—a cross for the eye line and T-zone, and shorter horizontal lines for the nose and mouth locations.

Step 3
Next lightly sketch the basic features—the eyes, ears, nose, mouth, eyebrows, and hairline. Try to sketch lightly, as darker lines are difficult to erase and may wear down the paper if you decide to redraw any features.

Step 4
When you are satisfied with your sketch, ink your drawing, or turn it into line art. Add the final details, such as eyelashes and pupils. Some artists color directly on a refined sketch; others clean and tighten them with line art first.

Step 5
The final step is colori. Whatever medium you decide to use here is completely up to you! See page 5 for colori techniques.

Drawing Hair

Curly, spiky, cropped, or straight—there are many different ways to draw hair and hairdos can be interpreted differently based on an artist's style. Some artists prefer drawing hair realistically with a lot of detail. Others prefer a stylized look, and draw only contour lines that imply the hair's shape. You can also block in the hair without highlights or shading if a character has dark hair. The choices are endless!

Hairstyles and Personality Hair can play an important role in defining a character. For example, you may give a bubbly, *shôjo* girl bouncy curls or a young, rebellious hero pointy, gravity-defying locks. Accentuate a tough guy's angular features with close-cropped hair, a widow's peak, and sideburns.

Hair textures

It is helpful to understand how individual strands and clumps of hair behave when trying to depict various hair textures and styles. Natural hair styles will have a different shape and weight than crimped, curled, or bluntly cut hair.

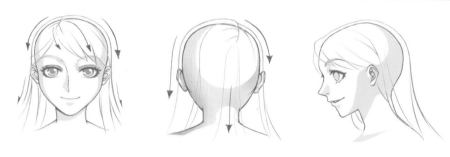

Hair and Gravity In this illustration, the hair is transparent, so you can see how hair drapes around the head and neck. Keep in mind that gravity determines how a character's hair falls. Decide where you want to part the hair (this example shows a side part) and draw the hair hanging down from that part.

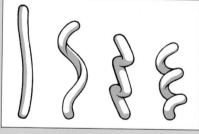

Manipulated Hair Imagine each strand of hair as a string. When straight, it is at its maximum length. Adding a wave, crimp, or curl shrinks the strand. Now remember that hair is made up of many individual strands.

Hair and Head Shape There is a close relationship between the skull, head, and hair. The shape of the skull defines the head shape and the head shape affects the size and direction of hair growth. Some characters have large hair styles or tie their hair back, and wind may influence the shape of hair. Always draw hair around the shape of the head and consider the effects of gravity.

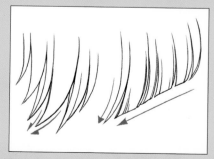

Hair Ends In most styles, hair ends are drawn in points or clumps (above, left). You also can draw hair that is cropped straight at the ends, giving the hair a freshly cut appearance (above, right).

Drawing Facial Features

A great deal of manga storytelling occurs on a character's face where a range of emotions are displayed. On page 8 you learned the basic proport and relationships between features. Now let's focus on the individual facial features and see how they all work together to bring a character to life.

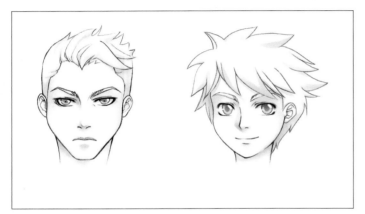

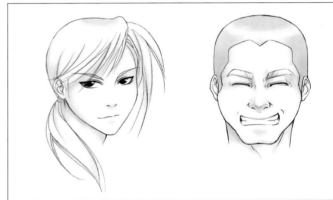

Eyes

Eyes are easily the most expressive part of a character's face, and there are an infinite number of ways to draw them. Above are a couple of basic examples of different eye shapes and sizes. Notice how the eyes draw your attention and define the character. The male with beady, narrow eyes could be a villain, and the big, bubbly eyes on the right could belong to a young boy in a *shōjo* comic. Try experimenting with a few different eye styles while thinking about the type of character you are trying to portray. Factors such as age, ethnicity, and personality can all affect the eyes.

Eyebrows

Eyebrows are also important for portraying expressions. Since eyebrows are made of hair, they will usually be the same color and style as a character's hair, although you can choose to give a little man huge, bushy, black eyebrows. Altering the shape of the eyebrow is effective for showin emotions. For example, if both eyebrows are facing sharply towards the center of the face, that would make the character look very angry. Having th point up may give the feeling of surprise or shock. You can use your own face as a reference—get in front of a mirror and start making faces, and pa attention to how your eyebrows move and shift with each one.

Noses and Mouths

Noses don't move the way mouths and eyes do, but they complete th overall symmetry of the face and add a bit of character. Some artists fi it difficult to draw noses, especially from the front view, but sometime just takes two small dots, short lines, or the implied shadow of the nos Also keep in mind that males tend to have more prominent noses. The mouth is what makes a character smile, frown, laugh, or shout. Like ey and noses, there are many ways to draw mouths—with simple lines or defined lips and dimples. On the other hand, some artists don't draw no at all. This is especially common in *chibi* drawings, where the nose play lesser role.

Angled Eyebrow   **Bushy Eyebrow**   **Arched Eyebrow**   **Thin, Rounded Eyebrow**   **Realistic Eyebrow**

Drawing Expressions Now put all of the facial features together to create different expressions. The character at left is shown making a variety of extreme faces—happiness, sadness, embarrassment, disapproval, outrage, fear, and wickedness. Even though the expressions change, the character should remain clearly recognizable in all drawings with consistent features, or readers may confuse him/her for different characters. A great exercise is to draw one character with many different emotions, making sure that he/she looks like the same character throughout.

Tip

The best way to practice expressions is to observe and draw from real life. If you have a friend who also likes to draw, one of you can make faces at the other while you quickly sketch them. You can also look to your favorite manga artists to see how they approach different emotions and expressions.

Head Shapes

The shape of a character's head can reveal a lot about the character's personality. While the most common head shape is an oval, there are many other possibilities. The three basic shapes for drawing anything are the circle, square, and triangle. Experiment by combining the different shapes to create more unique and expressive head shapes.

Oval Most of your characters will have oval-shaped heads.

Triangular Sharply angled heads are good for evil villains.

Square Give strong, beefy guys sturdy, square heads.

Circular Comical characters often have circular heads.

Full Figure Male

Understanding the human form is integral to becoming a manga artist, as human bodies are featured prominently in this character-driven art form. Below is a brief overview of a standard male form. While there are many types of male bodies—thin, overweight, or bulky—I generally like to draw relatively fit males with broad shoulders and slim waists. I also use angular lines, sharp muscle definition, and geometric shapes to convey strength and firmness. The guidelines below show how to use a character's head as a measuring unit. A standard figure's height is equal to seven of its heads. The proportions apply to the four major full-figure views—front, three-quarter, side, and back. Another general observation is that the male's upper body tends to be broader and wider than the lower body.

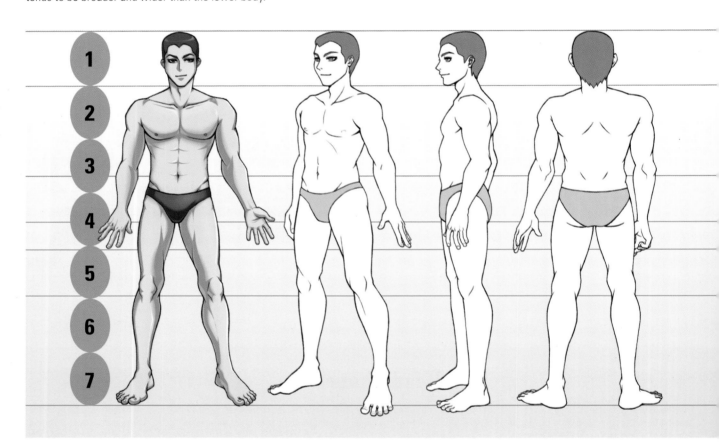

Foreshortened Male
When viewed from above, this male figure is *foreshortened*. The top of the head and shoulders are large, with the rest of the body drawn with increasingly shorter lines to convey depth and distance.

Sitting Male While you can draw the body in an infinite amount of poses, the actual length and size of any given body part never changes. This is where basic shapes and lines of action help guide you through complex proportions and poses.

Full Figure Female

For my particular style, I like to draw females with trim, firm, and fit bodies—not too thin or voluptuous. However, a character's figure also depends on er age; for example, adult women tend to have more prominent curves than teenage girls. While males are usually heavier in the upper body, females ave smoother, rounder contours—particularly in areas such as the chest and hips. Therefore, females generally carry more weight in their lower bodies. he female's height is also equivalent to seven of her heads. However, if you put the male and female figures side by side, the male is taller, because the emale's head is smaller, resulting in an overall shorter height.

eshortened Female As with the male re viewed from above, this female's lower y appears smaller and farther away.

Lounging Female In this pose, the female's heads and hands are closest to the viewer. Her lower body is smaller, as it's farther away, or foreshortened. She is also lying at an angle, which helps further define the foreshortening.

Different Body Types

Once you are comfortable using the basic rules of body proportions and foreshortening discussed on pages 12–13, you can draw any adult or young adult body type and pose. You can even choose to exaggerate bodies or tweak specific body parts (see page 15).

You may also want to create younger and older characters or characters that grow up during the course of your story. To depict characters of different ages, fundamental laws of proportion still apply. However, there are some important differences between the bodies of children and adults. Below is a character at different ages, from a baby to an adult woman. Notice how her head is much larger in proportion to her body as a child than as a teen and adult. Also notice that as she ages, her curves, as well as her muscles, become more defined. Males tend to develop muscles and broader shoulders as they age, also.

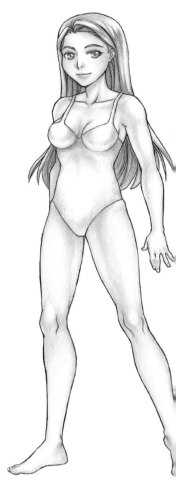

Baby	Child	Teen	Adult
At this stage, male and female babies often look similar, especially if you disregard characteristics that define gender, such as clothes. At birth, babies' heads are much larger in proportion to their bodies. Exaggerating this concept by making the head and eyes very large and the hands and feet very small helps emphasize the young age.	Young children tend to have baby fat, resulting in evenly shaped, rounded torsos, and carry a lot of baby fat and limbs without much definition. Take away things like clothes and hair, and gender can still be hard to distinguish. Like with babies, drawing larger eyes and bigger heads will convey a more childlike age.	In adolescence, fat disperses, and muscles and bone structure become more prominent. A teenage girl, for example, may have longer legs and a curvy body, but still maintain a slim waist and form, which can help define her youth. Eye size can shrink, which can help define aging and growing up.	As a fully grown adult, this character's bone structure, muscles, and "hourglass" shape are well-defined. She stands at her full seven-head height.

What's a Chibi?

A common drawing concept found in anime and manga is the "chibi" form. *Chibis* are generally smaller, simpler caricatures of characters that are used to illustrate light, comedic situations. The word "chibi" is Japanese for "short person" or "small child." However, that doesn't make a younger version of a character a *chibi*. The three figures below are *chibi* versions of the characters on page 9. They are portrayed in a simplified and light-hearted fashion. What makes them *chibi* rather than children is that they appear older than children, but are drawn in a cute, cartoon-like style. Any character can be drawn in *chibi* style—even the most menacing villains!

Elongated Chibi Not every *chibi* character has to be short and stout. You can create a variation of the *chibi* form by drawing big heads with thin, elongated bodies. The most prominent feature of a *chibi* is the disproportionately large head and eyes, as well as simplified facial features. Study your favorite manga to see how *chibis* are dealt with and be sure draw in a style that creates a mood appropriate to a comic *chibi* situation.

Exaggeration Now that you've learned the fundamentals of drawing bodies, you can experiment and learn how to bend the rules. Many manga artists employ exaggeration to achieve stronger, more prominent characteristics. One of the male figures at left is extremely muscular with heavily exaggerated facial features. The other character is a heavyweight sumo wrestler. If you removed all the muscle and fat from these two characters, their bodies would be similar in terms of bone structure. However, the muscular character is composed of mostly angular lines, and the sumo wrestler is round virtually all over. Their bodies and facial features make a bold statement about their personalities.

Male Hero

Most manga adventures feature a mysterious and moody hero with a serious but honorable goal or quest. This male hero may appear cold and distant, but he embodies the values of perseverance, fellowship, and justice.

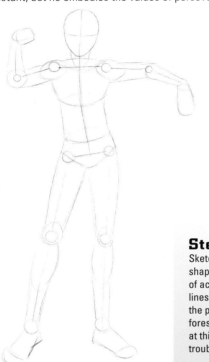

Step 1
Sketch the body with basic shapes and map out the line of action, hip and shoulder lines, and major joints. Finalize the pose, body proportions, foreshortening, and perspective at this stage to prevent troublesome revisions later on.

Step 2
Sketch the basic contours of the body and sword. Developing the body will help with clothing shapes and folds later. Working from the head down, add basic details in the hair, face, hands, and feet.

Step 3
Now add the clothes, but sketch lightly, as hard lines are difficult to erase and tend to smudge. Work in layers, drawing the shirt, coat, and pants. Next add accessories, such as the tie, pocket chain, and shoes.

Step 4
Once you have your final sketch you can ink your drawing to create line art or make in more permanent. Inking will force you to clean up your drawing, making it easier to scan or color over.

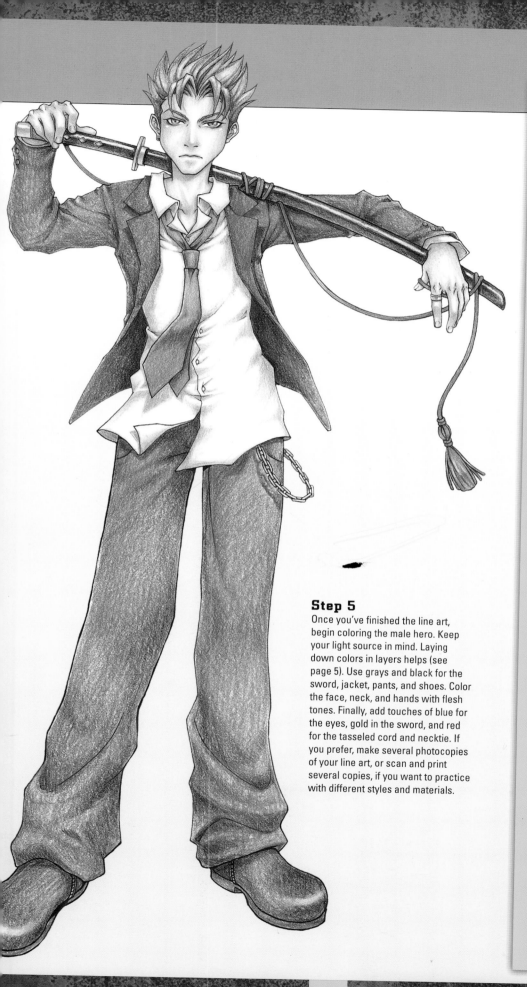

Finishing Techniques

Fine details and value contrasts can bring a character to life. Not all of the details have to be drawn in the line art; shapes, depth, and details can be rendered with coloring. See page 5 for more information on inking, shading, and coloring.

Details In the line art, the major details have been drawn in, but the nose is only represented with nostrils.

Layers Color in layers, starting with the lightest colors and gradually building up darker colors.

Shadows and Highlights Create sharper contrasts by darkening shadows and brightening highlights.

Step 5

Once you've finished the line art, begin coloring the male hero. Keep your light source in mind. Laying down colors in layers helps (see page 5). Use grays and black for the sword, jacket, pants, and shoes. Color the face, neck, and hands with flesh tones. Finally, add touches of blue for the eyes, gold in the sword, and red for the tasseled cord and necktie. If you prefer, make several photocopies of your line art, or scan and print several copies, if you want to practice with different styles and materials.

School Girl

Shôjo manga often revolve around the daily lives of junior high or high school students. This school girl's main concerns involve passing her classe, finding romance, and bonding with her girlfriends. She may have hidden super powers, but that's for you, the *mangaka*, to decide!

Step 1

First, sketch out the basic shapes for this casual pose. Be sure to establish the action, shoulder, and hip lines, place the major joints, and measure out accurate body proportions.

Step 2

Draw the basic contours of the body, hair, and handbag. Next, add her facial features. Think about the character's personality. This classic girl next door has straight hair and wide, innocent eyes.

Step 3

Now draw her clothing. A traditional Japanese school uniform includes a collared shirt, tie, sweater, and short pleated skirt. To complete the outfit, add accessories, such as hairpins, a watch, plush keychain, and shoes. Be sure to render your final details and textures at this stage.

Step 4

Ink the sketch and erase unnecessary marks. Use fine, thin lines for a light, cheerful mood. You may want to make copies of your inked drawing to practice coloring on and work out your color palette before applying color to your line art.

Expressive Accessories

Like hair, facial features, and body type, accessories tell a story as well. The school girl's bookbag, plush bunny, and hair clips show her youthful innocence. Below, see how jewelry, weapons, and other accessories add character.

Pet Lover This young girl's collar and bell strongly identify her with the animals that she adores.

Bad Boy Something as tiny as an earring can give this confident bad boy a bit of unconventional charm.

Fighter A deadly ninja star, sleek sword, or classic pistol reflects a character's fighting style.

Step 5

Begin coloring by laying down the lightest colors first, and then build up the darkest areas. If you are working with markers, use light pressure. Try using a cool gray for the sweater and a warmer gray or brown for the bag. With soft strokes, capture the textures in the blue skirt and strands of brown hair. Color the tie red and add pink for the hair pins, watchband, and shoes. Finish up by adding a few key highlights with a white gel pen or white acrylic paint. Adding white dots to the eyes and jewelry make them look brighter and shinier.

Ninja

Now that we've covered everyday characters, such as the school girl and the male hero, you may want to try out something more dynamic and complex. A ninja is a great character to experiment with, as ninjas are expert assassins and have extremely agile movements and action-packed live

Step 1

Begin with the basic shapes and lines of action. For this ninja, it may be harder to see the line of action and joints because of the extreme pose. Keep in mind that arms and legs don't shrink in length though foreshortening (see page 12–13) makes it look like they do. Experiment at this stage to find a really dynamic pose.

Step 2

Sketch the contours of the body, and add the facial features. I drew in the entire face here so the expression would be clearly defined. Shape out the muscles, fingers, and legs. With an action pose, you want to review your sketch often to see if it looks awkward or if the pose looks too stiff. You can always ask a friend to pose for you or keep a mirror handy.

Step 3

Draw the basic clothing and accessories, including weapons, sandals, and spiked gauntlets. Carefully render the different folds and textures. Although his face will be covered, I suggest sketching the ninja's facial features to establish his personality and expression.

Step 4

Now ink your final drawing, sharpening up the details. As this image involves many distinct elements that are close together, be cautious about smudging. You can place a small ruler or plastic lid beneath your hand to prevent the oils on your skin from smearing your work.

Step 5
The color palette for a ninja is basically monochromatic. His clothing, sword, eyebrows, and mask are very dark gray and black. Color the band around his leg a dark brown and let the lighter flesh tones of his fingers and area around his eyes provide a dramatic contrast to his dark apparel. Next, add silver accents to his armor, spikes, headband, and *shuriken*, or throwing star. Complete the image with piercing blue eyes, and remember to leave bright highlights in the eyes and reflective metal items.

Basic Manga Principles

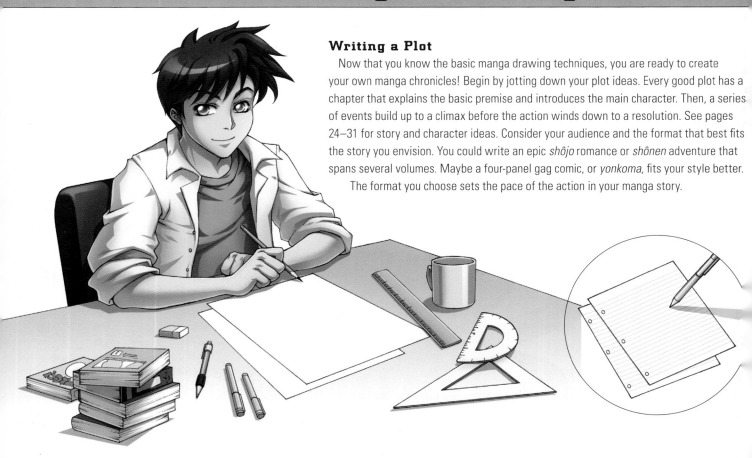

Writing a Plot

Now that you know the basic manga drawing techniques, you are ready to create your own manga chronicles! Begin by jotting down your plot ideas. Every good plot has a chapter that explains the basic premise and introduces the main character. Then, a series of events build up to a climax before the action winds down to a resolution. See pages 24–31 for story and character ideas. Consider your audience and the format that best fits the story you envision. You could write an epic *shôjo* romance or *shônen* adventure that spans several volumes. Maybe a four-panel gag comic, or *yonkoma*, fits your style better. The format you choose sets the pace of the action in your manga story.

Scriptwriting and Thumbnailing

Once you have a plot, script the scenes of your manga, fleshing out scenes, sound effects, and dialogue. Next create thumbnails, or miniature sketches of pages where you plan panel layouts and character expressions. (See how the script below can be thumbnailed in the example at right.) Thumbnailing can occur during or after scriptwriting. The thumbnailing process is similar to storyboarding a movie, but you have more freedom with panel shapes and sizes.

When laying out a scene, think of yourself as a movie director who uses different camera angles—such as the bird's eye view, close-up, or low-angle shot—to set specific moods. Your stage direction will enable readers to easily follow transitions between panels and dialogue balloons.

Feel free to experiment with different panel layouts for a single scene to discover what works best.

PAGE 1

Panel 1: [Exterior shot of a high school]

Panel 2: [Close-up of a school girl's running feet]

Sound Effect: TP TP TP TP

Panel 3: [Full front shot of school girl running, looking stressed out because she is late for class]

Panel 4: [Close-up of watch on girl's right wrist]

Girl thinking: I can make it!

Panel 5: [Profile view of girl sprinting towards the school gate, with speed lines to indicate how fast she is moving. Determined expression on girl's face.]

Girl thinking: I CAN'T BE LATE!

enciling and Inking

ith your script, thumbnails, and drawing materials on hand, you are ready to bring your manga
ry to life! Using the tips and techniques you learned in the drawing lessons and projects in this
k, start pencilling your manga.

s the majority of manga is printed in black and white—with the exception of covers and
asional chapter-opening pages in color—you will finalize most of your artwork in ink. Use a
-tipped black marker to ink your pencil drawings, or try other types of pens to achieve different
ects. Notice how the lines in the image at right vary in weight (or thickness), defining a range of
tures. Practice creating different types of lines on scratch paper with your pen before inking
r manga. (See pages 3 and 5 for more on pens and inking.)

 Step 1 Looking to your thumbnail as a reference, begin by using your ruler and pencil to draw in the panel borders.

 **Step 2** Sketch in the basic shapes and features in each panel—don't forget to include word balloons.

 **Step 3** Add details and finish your pencil work. Finally, ink your drawings, tightening up images even further.

ecial Effects

ump up the action in your manga with sound effects and dynamic visual cues. Write
"CRASH!!" in bold caps that illustrate the deafening roar of an impact or draw a burst
t captures the power of an explosion. You can also draw multiple parallel lines to
cate speed. Adding special effects draws the reader deeper into your manga story.

I AM A SPEECH BUBBLE.

I AM A SPEECH BUBBLE.

Lettering

Although manga is largely visual storytelling, you must also handle the text with care. With the ruler and pencil, lightly draw guidelines in the speech bubble, and then pencil in the dialogue. After you've worked out the letter spacing in pencil, ink over the words. Another option is to type out the words on the computer. You can try different fonts and paste the text into the word bubbles.

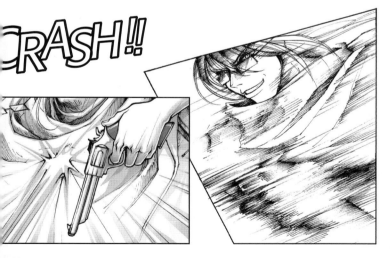

nishing Your Manga Page

fter inking, grab your eraser and clean up visible pencil lines, rubbing gently to
vent the paper from wrinkling. Next, add shading and texture with screentones.
w sit back and admire your finished manga page. You have completed the first
to becoming a *mangaka!*

or more manga madness, try using ink washes. Another finishing technique is to
n your inked page and add digital screentones and digital lettering on the
puter. There are many techniques available for refining your manga pages and
ting your own visual style, and I encourage you to explore all of them.

Choose Your Own Adventure

Sometimes it's difficult to start creating your own manga, even with all of the basic manga principles u your belt, because there are so many genres to choose from. If you're not really sure where to begin, it ma help to think about what type of manga you like t read. Take the quiz on the opposite page to disc your manga style and story ideas that may jumpstart your manga imagination!

What kind of otaku are you?

An *otaku* is a serious manga fan. Answer these questions to figure out what manga style suits you best.

) My favorite mangas make me

Sweat

Cry

Laugh

All of the above

) My favorite thing to do when I come home is

Playing my favorite video game—one that involves tons of action!

Calling up my friends or girlfriend/boyfriend to chat.

Cooking, listening to music, or working out.

I love doing all of these activities. It just depends on my mood.

If I had super powers, I would use them to

Lead an elite fighting squad to save the world.

Prevent evil and heal wounded hearts.

Win tournaments and spread my favorite activities across the world.

I can't decide. There are too many things I would do!

I am more of a

Fighter

Lover

Doer

All of the above

5.) My bedroom walls are plastered with

A. Life-sized posters of all my favorite heroes.

B. Photos of my friends and family, animal pictures, floral decorations, or cool designs.

C. Posters of my favorite sports teams or bands.

D. All of the above

6.) At the mall, you'd most likely find me in a(n)

A. Electronics or game store

B. Accessories, clothing, or pet store

C. Music, sporting goods, or kitchen goods store

D. Department store—it has everything!

7.) I can best be described as

A. Adventurous

B. Sentimental

C. Enthusiastic

D. All of the above

8.) If I was a manga character, I would be

A. A samurai or space warrior

B. A magical girl or star-crossed lover

C. A talented hero

D. Every character

Results: If you got…

Mostly A's:

You're a *Heroic Otaku*. You value friendship, perseverance, and victory, and you love adventure, martial arts, and stories that cross the universe. Throw in some robots and a few monsters, and you have the perfect manga! Consider using a ninja in your next story or set your characters on a strange planet filled with dragons, wizards, and fantastical creatures.

Mostly B's:

You're a *Romantic Otaku*. You love falling in love and can't resist getting swept up in stories that feature magical girls, young heroes, and couples in love. Close relationships, happiness, and personal style are important to you. Try creating an epic romance set during your favorite historical period or focus on the daily dramas all around you—but with a magical twist!

Mostly C's:

You're a *Hobbyist Otaku*. You're passionate about sports, games, performance art, and food, so stories featuring these popular pastimes are sure to get you daydreaming. For added drama, check out board game manga or cook up a tale revolving around an extreme version of your favorite activity.

Mostly D's:

You're an *Eclectic Otaku*. You love all forms of manga and can't get enough of them. Consider adding a pet or fun animal mascot to your stories or create quirky characters with different specialties that allow you to express all of your varied interests. The possibilities are endless!

Manga Meet & Greet

The types of characters that populate the manga world are vast and varied, ranging from magical girls who lead secret lives to sinister villains who constantly challenge our courageous heroes. Knowing the genre of manga that appeals to you—heroic, romantic, hobbyist, or eclectic—can help narrow down your character options. First decide on your protagonist, and then think about his/her relationships with the other characters in your story.

A compelling story follows a protagonist through a journey of discovery and personal progress, whether the protagonist is a hero on an epic quest or an ordinary student dealing with daily life. Each character in the story contributes to the protagonist's development and may act as an ally, rival, love interest, or enemy. You may also choose to focus on more than one protagonist or add characters for the sole purpose of comic relief. Regardless of your character choices, be sure to portray them in situations that bring out their most prominent personality traits, involve a lot of interaction, and allow them to affect each other's character growth.

Cat Girl Are you a feline lover? Add the purr-fect touch to your manga with a cat girl, a common character whose origins can be traced back to the transforming cat of Japanese folklore.

Chibis Draw *chibi* versions of your characters for comedic scenes or make all of your characters adorable *chibis!*

Animals Include cute mascots, animal familiars, or giant talking creatures in your story. You can also center the drama on the bond between a character and his/her pet.

Heroes and Villains Popular heroes and villains include ninjas, vampires, and knights. Pit your characters against each other for action-packed drama!

Magical Girl ...scinated by the ...ea of secret ...entities? Feature ...high school girl ...ho transforms into ...magical heroine!

Maid Many romantic comedies pair up attractive maids with ordinary guys. Add a twist to this convention with a bookish or clumsy maid.

Otaku An *otaku* is a fan of anything, from video games to manga. Use an *otaku* character to show how an average, geeky guy can win romance and recognition with his kind heart.

Finding Inspiration from Real Lif

SNACKS

POPCORN $4.00
SODA $2.00
HOT DOGS $2.00
COTTON CANDY . $2.00
PIZZA $3.00

POPCORN   HOT DOGS

Most artists draw upon their own experiences and feelings to find inspirati
for their art. Try creating a love story that is based upon your own romantic
experiences or a fantastical story that brings your most serious or silliest hop
to life. You can also manga-fy a friend's eventful life.

Another great way to come up with storylines and characters is to look aro
you for inspiration. Ordinary people that you see and come into contact with
can spur intriguing characters. Take time to simply observe people and imagi
what their stories are.

Average Family A young couple and their daughter enjoy a fun outing at the local fair.

Little Girl This sweet girl just won a stuffed animal at the ring toss.

Young Woman A pr
fairgoer asks the frien
officer for directions.

Police Officer Perhaps this handsome officer practices martial arts in his spare time.

Teenage Couple This young couple in love could be the captain of the football team and the head cheerleader.

Manga-fy This!

Now transform the everyday people you see into popular manga characters. Tap into the manga potential of your family members, friends, classmates, and coworkers. It's *your* manga-verse, so let your imagination run wild! The characters that inhabit the pages of your manga are totally up to you, but you can borrow traits and inspiration from the people around you.

Animal Familiar A plush toy car become an energetic side-kick!

Superhero Family The ordinary family from the fair scene has been completely revamped into an intergalactic crime-fighting team, complete with futuristic outfits and cool gadgets.

Imperial Agent
An ordinary girl can be transformed into a miko, or shrine maiden—a priestess with immense spiritual energy who can convey fortunes and futures from ancient gods.

Samurai This warrior follows a strict code of honor and service, similar to his modern-day counterpart, the police officer.

Royal Couple Do you recognize this dashing prince and his pampered princess? They are the sweet teenage couple on a date at the fair.

Conquer the Manga-Verse

Congratulations! You are well on your way to becoming a *mangaka*. The basic tools, techniques, and tips in this kit were designed to introduce you to the art of manga and encourage you to create your own manga stories. However, your manga journey has just begun! To develop your newfound skills, I recommend drawing every day. Experiment with different styles, subject matter, and drawing materials. Simply carry your sketchbook with you everywhere, and practice drawing the people and objects around you. Remember, your favorite manga and movies, your own experiences, and just about anything can be a source of inspiration.

So I entrust you with this mission: Go out into the world and spread the manga madness!